# italian

# italian

EASY, DELICIOUS DISHES FOR FAMILY AND FRIENDS

foreword by
valentina harris

**southwater**

This edition is published by Southwater
Southwater is an imprint of Anness Publishing Ltd
Hermes House, 88–89 Blackfriars Road, London SE1 8HA
tel. 020 7401 2077; fax 020 7633 9499
www.southwaterbooks.com; info@anness.com
© Anness Publishing Ltd 1996, 2004

UK agent: The Manning Partnership Ltd, 6 The Old Dairy, Melcombe Road, Bath BA2 3LR; tel. 01225 478444; fax 01225 478440;
sales@manning-partnership.co.uk
UK distributor: Grantham Book Services Ltd, Isaac Newton Way, Alma Park Industrial Estate, Grantham, Lincs NG31 9SD; tel. 01476 541080; fax
01476 541061; orders@gbs.tbs-ltd.co.uk
North American agent/distributor: National Book Network, 4501 Forbes Boulevard, Suite 200, Lanham, MD 20706; tel. 301 459 3366;
fax 301 429 5746; www.nbnbooks.com
Australian agent/distributor: Pan Macmillan Australia, Level 18, St Martins Tower, 31 Market St, Sydney, NSW 2000; tel. 1300 135 113;
fax 1300 135 103; customer.service@macmillan.com.au
New Zealand agent/distributor: David Bateman Ltd, 30 Tarndale Grove, Off Bush Road, Albany, Auckland; tel. (09) 415 7664; fax (09) 415 8892

A CIP catalogue record for this book is available from the British Library.

*Publisher* Joanna Lorenz
*Senior Cookery Editor* Linda Fraser
*Cookery Editor* Anne Hildyard
*Designer* Nigel Partridge
*Illustrations* Madeleine David
*Photographers* Karl Adamson, Edward Allwright, Steve Baxter, James Duncan, Amanda Heywood and Michael Michaels
*Recipes* Carla Capalbo, Roz Denny, Sarah Gates, Shirley Gill, Norma Macmillan, Annie Nichols and Laura Washburn
*Food for photography* Beverly Le Blanc, Elizabeth Wolf-Cohen, Marilyn Forbes, Wallace Heim,
Wendy Lee, Jenny Shapter and Jane Stevenson
*Stylists* Madelaine Brehaut, Carla Capalbo, Hilary Guy, Amanda Heywood, Blake Minton and Kirsty Rawlings
*Cover Photography* Nicki Dowey, *Food Stylist* Emma Patmore, *Design* Wilson Harvey
Previously published as part of the *Classic* cookery series

1 3 5 7 9 10 8 6 4 2

For all recipes, quantities are given in both metric and imperial measures, and, where appropriate, measures are also given in
standard cups and spoons. Follow one set, but not a mixture, because they are not interchangeable.

Picture on frontispiece and page 8: Zefa Pictures Ltd. Pictures on page 7 and page 9: John Freeman

# CONTENTS

# FOREWORD

In my travels around the world as a self-styled spokesperson for the glories of the Italian kitchen and the Italian wine cellar, it is a constant delight to me just how popular Italian food is. Whether I am in Cape Town or teaching a group of Australians in Sicily, the enthusiasm with which every Italian recipe is met seems boundless.

I think this has to do principally with three basic truths: one: it is relatively cheap to buy the ingredients required for Italian recipes; two: by and large (with some notable exceptions, I grant you) Italian food is fairly low in fats and therefore healthy; three: it is very easy to cook Italian food *well*. No great techniques need to be mastered for the preparation of authentic Italian food, it is a style of cooking which relies far too heavily on that most elusive cook's skill: instinct! In all my years as a teacher of Italian regional cuisine, I have learned that what makes a very good cook become an excellent cook is the self-confidence to bring your instinct into play –  then you'll just *know* how much more salt and pepper is required, whether the dish requires just a few minutes longer in the oven, or if a moment longer in the pan is going to toughen the meat you're cooking.

One of the best ways to develop that confidence is by collecting lots of recipe books with dishes which you enjoy. You can constantly refer to them and they'll become your best friends in the kitchen. I know for certain that nobody who cooks with passion can ever have enough cookery books, and personally, I can never own enough books about Italian cookery, even though I have made it my life for the past 20 years. So I welcome this one to my shelf!

Happy cooking and *Felicita in Cucina*!

VALENTINA HARRIS

# INTRODUCTION

Italian food is imaginative, colourful and bursting with flavour. It is in harmony with today's thoughts on healthy eating and the "Mediterranean diet", with its emphasis on energy-giving foods, olive oil and plenty of fruit and vegetables. Italy is a country of changing climates and landscapes, and so too is its cooking, varying according to the region from which a particular dish comes. From the cool and mountainous north come hearty, warming dishes. Among these are polenta, a gorgeous, golden yellow porridge made from cornmeal; wonderful baked pasta dishes such as lasagne; and rich risottos, with locally grown arborio rice, of which northern

Italians eat rather a lot. From the south, where the climate is warmer, we find more colourful, dishes, such as pizza and simple meat dishes made with additional ingredients such as peppers, olives and herbs that thrive in the hot Mediterranean sun. Southern Italians like their pasta served simply; with oil, and herbs.

The land is rich in produce: from the forests come game; sheep and goats graze in the foothills; wheat for pasta grows in the plains; and there is a wealth of vegetables and fruit in every field and orchard. Veal, beef and dairy foods are produced, the seas and lakes are brimming with all sorts of fish and shellfish, and in the hills, vines and olive trees are cultivated.

Olive oil is one of the most important ingredients in Italian cooking and although it may seem expensive, it pays to use the best that you can afford. Most recipes only need a little and it makes all the difference to the flavour of a dish. Extra virgin olive oil, produced from the first cold pressing of the olives, is excellent for dressings or pouring on to pasta, while pure olive oil is perfect for cooking.

Vegetables play a vital role in Italian cuisine and among those most often used are courgettes, aubergines, broccoli, peppers, spinach and tomatoes. Other favourite Italian ingredients include garlic, freshly grated nutmeg, capers, olives and pine nuts, all adding enticing flavours to savoury dishes.

*Fish and seafood in a street market in Venice (left), a display of freshly baked pastries and biscuits (right), and a colourful roadside stall selling lemons, dried red chillies, nuts and cherries (far right), show just a small selection of Italy's tempting produce.*

Cheese is used in small amounts as an ingredient in many recipes. Italians make a large variety of cheeses and these are becoming increasingly easier to find in other countries. There are many varieties of cheese ranging from soft, crumbly and mild, to hard, creamy and full-flavoured. The most well-known is Parmesan, the undisputed king of Italian cheeses. Genuine Parmesan cheese is only made in Emilia and an authentic cheese always has the title "Parmigiano-Reggiano" stamped on its rind. Always buy fresh Parmesan for grating – the flavour of ready-grated Parmesan is a poor substitute.

Italian food is simple and rustic, lovingly prepared and well-presented. Cooking as the Italians do is easy and fun. They love to cook, but above all, Italians enjoy sharing food with friends and family, turning even the simplest meal into a celebration. With the help of these delicious and authentic recipes, you will be certain to do the same.

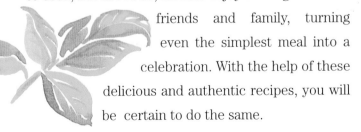

# MINESTRONE WITH PESTO
### Minestrone con Pesto

inestrone is a substantial mixed vegetable soup made with almost any combination of fresh seasonal vegetables. Short pasta or rice may also be added. This version includes pesto sauce.

### INGREDIENTS
*1.5 litres/2½ pints/6¼ cups stock or water,*
*or a combination of both*
*45ml/3 tbsp olive oil*
*1 large onion, finely chopped*
*1 leek, sliced*
*2 carrots, finely chopped*
*1 celery stick, finely chopped*
*2 garlic cloves, finely chopped*
*2 potatoes, peeled and cut into small dice*
*1 bay leaf*
*1 sprig fresh thyme, or 1.5ml/¼ tsp*
*dried thyme*
*115g/4oz/¾ cup peas, fresh or frozen*
*2–3 courgettes, finely chopped*
*3 tomatoes, peeled and finely chopped*
*425g/15oz/2 cups cooked or canned*
*beans, such as cannellini*
*45ml/3 tbsp pesto sauce*
*freshly grated Parmesan cheese, to serve*
*salt and ground black pepper*

*SERVES 6*

1 In a large saucepan, heat the stock or water until it reaches simmering point.

2 In another saucepan heat the olive oil. Stir in the onion and leek, and cook for 5–6 minutes, or until the onion softens.

3 Add the carrots, celery and garlic, and cook over a moderate heat, stirring often, for a further 5 minutes. Add the potatoes and cook for a further 2–3 minutes.

4 Pour in the hot stock or water, and stir well. Add the bay leaf and thyme and season with salt and pepper. Bring to the boil, then reduce the heat slightly, and leave to cook for 10–12 minutes more.

5 Stir in the peas, if fresh, and the finely chopped courgettes and simmer for a further 5 minutes. Add the frozen peas, if using, and the chopped tomatoes. Cover the pan, bring slowly to the boil, then simmer the mixture for about 5–8 minutes.

6 About 20 minutes before serving the minestrone, remove the lid, and stir in the beans. Simmer for 10 minutes. Stir in the pesto sauce. Taste and adjust the seasoning if necessary. Simmer for a further 5 minutes, then remove the pan from the heat. Allow the soup to stand for a few minutes, to bring out the flavours, then serve in warmed bowls. Serve the grated Parmesan separately.

# EGG AND CHEESE SOUP

*Stracciatella*

I n this classic Roman soup, eggs and cheese are beaten into hot stock, producing a slightly "curdled" texture characteristic of the dish.

### INGREDIENTS
*3 eggs*
*45ml/3 tbsp fine semolina*
*90ml/6 tbsp freshly grated*
*Parmesan cheese*
*pinch of nutmeg*
*1.5 litres/2¹/₂ pints/6¹/₄ cups cold meat or*
*chicken stock*
*salt and ground black pepper*
*12 rounds of French bread, to serve*

*SERVES 6*

---

### COOK'S TIP
To avoid the soup curdling too much, don't allow the stock to start boiling after you have added the egg mixture.

1 Break the eggs into a bowl, then add the semolina and Parmesan cheese and beat together with a fork or wire whisk. Stir in the nutmeg. Beat in 250ml/8fl oz/1 cup of the meat or chicken stock. Set aside.

2 Meanwhile, pour the remaining stock into a large saucepan and heat gently for a few minutes, stirring occasionally, until the stock reaches simmering point.

3 When the stock is hot, a few minutes before you are ready to serve the soup, whisk the egg mixture into the stock. Raise the heat slightly, and bring it barely to the boil. Season with the salt and pepper. Cook for 3–4 minutes. As the egg cooks, the soup will not be completely smooth.

4 To serve, toast the rounds of French bread on both sides and place two in each soup bowl. Ladle the hot soup over the bread and serve immediately.

# MEDITERRANEAN GARLIC TOAST

*Bruschetta con Peperoni*

**M**editerranean garlic toast, or *bruschetta*, is served as a starter in Spain, Greece and Italy. With a topping of plum tomatoes, mozzarella and pepperoni, it also makes a filling snack.

INGREDIENTS

150g/5oz mozzarella, drained
2 plum tomatoes
½ French loaf
1 garlic clove, halved
30ml/2 tbsp olive oil, plus extra
for brushing
12 pepperoni slices
15ml/1 tbsp fresh torn basil, or 5ml/1 tsp
dried basil
salt and ground black pepper
fresh basil sprigs, to garnish

*SERVES 4*

**1** Preheat the grill to a medium heat. Cut the mozzarella into twelve slices and each tomato into six slices. Cut the French loaf in half and slice each half horizontally.

**2** Place the bread under the grill, cut side up, and toast lightly. While the bread is warm, rub the cut sides of the garlic clove on the toasted sides of the bread, then drizzle over about 7.5ml/½ tbsp of the oil.

**3** Top each toast with three slices of pepperoni, three slices of mozzarella and three slices of tomato (*left*). Brush the tops with a little more olive oil, and season well, and sprinkle over the basil.

**4** Return the toasts to the grill and toast for 2–3 minutes, until the cheese has melted. Remove and serve hot, garnished with sprigs of fresh basil.

# BRUSCHETTA WITH TOMATO

*Bruschetta con Pomodoro*

simple version of *bruschetta*, this tomato-topped toast may be served as a starter, a snack, or as an accompaniment to a meal.

### INGREDIENTS
*3–4 tomatoes, chopped*
*a few fresh basil leaves, torn into pieces*
*8 slices crusty white bread*
*2–3 garlic cloves, halved*
*90ml/6 tbsp extra virgin olive oil*
*salt and ground black pepper*

SERVES 4

1 Place the chopped tomatoes with their juice in a small bowl. Season with salt and pepper, and stir in the basil. Allow to stand for 10 minutes.

2 Toast or grill the bread until it is crisp on both sides. While it is still warm, rub one side of each piece of toast with the cut sides of the garlic.

3 Arrange the toasts on a serving platter, garlic side up, and sprinkle with the olive oil. Spoon on the chopped tomatoes, and serve immediately.

# PROSCIUTTO WITH FIGS

*Prosciutto con Fichi*

The hams cured in the region of Parma in northern Italy are held to be the finest in the country. Prosciutto makes an excellent starter when sliced paper-thin and served with fresh figs.

INGREDIENTS
*12 paper-thin slices prosciutto*
*8 ripe green or black figs*
*crusty bread and unsalted butter, to serve*

SERVES 4

1 Separate the slices of prosciutto and arrange them decoratively, in a spiral pattern, on a large serving platter.

2 Wipe the figs with a damp cloth. Cut them almost into quarters but do not cut all the way through the base. If the skins are tender, they may be eaten along with the inner fruit.

3 Arrange the quartered figs on top of the slices of prosciutto. Serve immediately with a basket of crusty country bread and pats of unsalted butter. Alternatively, serve with grissini, the Italian bread sticks, or warmed ciabatta rolls.

# CARPACCIO WITH ROCKET

*Carpaccio con Rucola*

arpaccio is a fine dish of raw beef marinated in lemon juice and olive oil. It is traditionally served with flakes of fresh Parmesan cheese. Use very fresh meat of the best quality.

### INGREDIENTS
*1 garlic clove, halved*
*1½ lemons*
*50ml/2fl oz/¼ cup extra virgin olive oil*
*2 bunches rocket*
*4 very thin slices of beef top round*
*salt and ground black pepper*
*115g/4oz/1 cup Parmesan cheese, thinly shaved, to serve*

### SERVES 4

1 Rub a small bowl all over with the cut side of the garlic. Squeeze the lemon juice into the bowl. Whisk in the olive oil and season with salt and pepper. Allow to stand for at least 15 minutes before using.

2 Carefully wash the rocket and tear off any thick stalks. Spin the leaves in a salad spinner or pat dry. Arrange the rocket around the edge of a serving platter, or divide among four individual plates.

3 Place the beef in the centre of the platter, and pour on the dressing, spreading it evenly over the meat. Arrange the shaved Parmesan on top of the meat slices and serve at once.

# AVOCADO, TOMATO AND MOZZARELLA PASTA SALAD

## *Insalata di Avocado, Pomodori e Mozzarella*

 stylish, summer salad made from ingredients representing the three colours of the Italian flag – a sunny cheerful dish!

### INGREDIENTS
*175g/6oz pasta bows (farfalle)*
*6 ripe red tomatoes*
*225g/8oz mozzarella*
*1 large ripe avocado*
*30ml/2 tbsp pine nuts, toasted*
*1 fresh basil sprig, to garnish*

### FOR THE DRESSING
*90ml/6 tbsp olive oil*
*30ml/2 tbsp wine vinegar*
*5ml/1 tsp balsamic vinegar (optional)*
*5ml/1 tsp wholegrain mustard*
*pinch of sugar*
*salt and ground black pepper*
*30ml/2 tbsp chopped fresh basil*

### SERVES 4

1 Cook the pasta in plenty of boiling salted water according to the manufacturer's instructions. Drain well and cool.

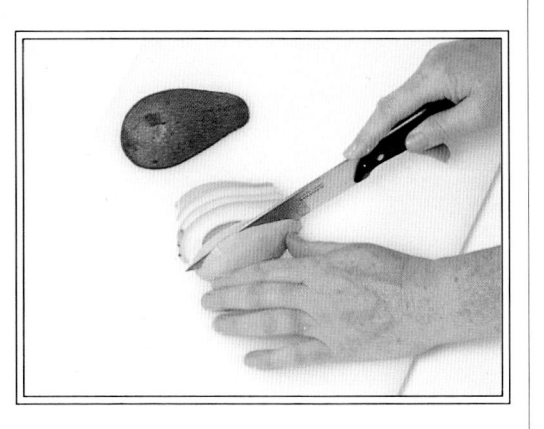

2 Slice the tomatoes and mozzarella into thin rounds. Halve the avocado, remove the stone, and peel off the skin. Slice the flesh lengthways.

3 Whisk together all the dressing ingredients, except the chopped fresh basil, in a small bowl.

4 Just before you are ready to serve the salad, arrange alternate slices of tomato, mozzarella and avocado in a spiral pattern, just slightly overlapping one another, around the edge of a large serving platter.

5 Toss the pasta with half the dressing and the chopped basil. Pile into the centre of the platter. Pour over the remaining dressing, scatter over the pine nuts and garnish the pasta with a sprig of fresh basil. Serve immediately.

---

### COOK'S TIP
To ripen avocados, put them into a paper bag with an apple or potato and leave in a warm place for 2–3 days.

---

# ROCKET AND PEAR SALAD

*Insalata di Rucola e Pere*

1 Peel and core the pears and slice thickly lengthways. Moisten the flesh with lemon juice to keep it white.

2 Combine the nut oil with the pears. Add the rocket leaves and toss.

3 Turn the salad out on to four small plates and top with shavings of Parmesan cheese. Season with freshly ground black pepper and serve with the bread.

For a sophisticated start to an elaborate meal, try this simple salad of honey-rich pears, fresh Parmesan and aromatic leaves of rocket. Enjoy it with a young Beaujolais or chilled Lambrusco wine.

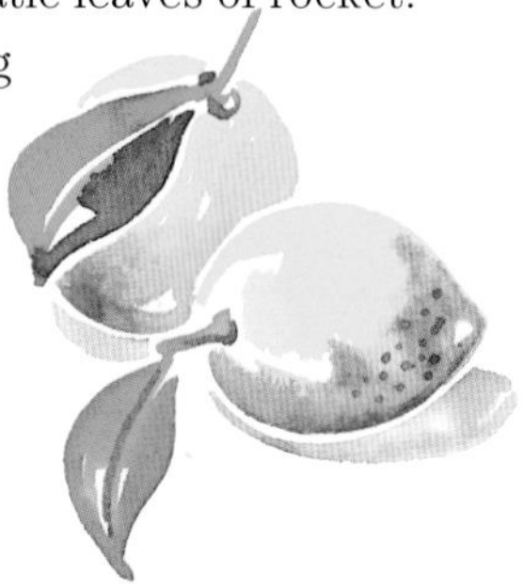

## INGREDIENTS

*3 ripe pears, Williams or Packhams*
*10ml/2 tsp lemon juice*
*45ml/3 tbsp hazelnut or walnut oil*
*115g/4oz rocket, washed and dried*
*75g/3oz Parmesan cheese, shaved*
*ground black pepper*
*open-textured bread, to serve*

*SERVES 4*

### COOK'S TIP
Rocket is fairly easy to find in supermarkets, but if you have a garden, then you can grow your own from early spring to late summer.

SOUPS, STARTERS AND SALADS

# BRESAOLA AND ONION SALAD

*Insalata di Bresaola e Cipolle*

B resaola is raw beef which has been salted in much the same way as *prosciutto di Parma*. In this flavourful salad, it is combined with the sweetness of juicy onions.

### INGREDIENTS

*2 medium onions, peeled*
*75–90ml/5–6 tbsp olive oil*
*juice of 1 lemon*
*12 thin slices bresaola*
*75g/3oz rocket, washed and dried*
*salt and ground black pepper*

*SERVES 4*

1 Slice each onion into eight wedges through the root. Arrange the wedges in a single layer in a flameproof dish. Brush them with a little of the olive oil and season well with salt and black pepper to taste.

2 Place the onion wedges under a hot grill and cook for about 8–10 minutes, turning once, until they are just beginning to soften and turn golden brown at the edges.

3 Meanwhile, to make the dressing, mix together the lemon juice and 60ml/4 tbsp of the olive oil. Add salt and black pepper to taste and whisk until thoroughly blended.

4 Pour the lemon dressing over the hot onions, mix well to coat the onions and leave until cold.

5 When the onions are cold, divide the bresaola slices among four individual serving plates and arrange the onions and rocket on top. Spoon over any remaining dressing and serve the salad immediately.

# TOMATO AND BREAD SALAD

*Panzanella*

This salad is a traditional peasant dish from Tuscany which was created to use up bread that was several days old. It is best made with sun-ripened tomatoes.

INGREDIENTS

400g/14oz/3½ cups stale white or brown
bread or rolls
4 large tomatoes
1 large red onion, or 6 spring onions
a few fresh basil leaves, to garnish

FOR THE DRESSING
60ml/4 tbsp extra virgin olive oil
30ml/2 tbsp white wine vinegar
salt and ground black pepper

*SERVES 4*

1 Cut the bread or rolls into thick slices. Place in a shallow bowl, and soak with cold water. Leave for at least 30 minutes.

2 Cut the tomatoes into chunks. Place in a serving bowl. Finely slice the onion or spring onions, and add them. Squeeze the water out of the bread and add the bread to the onions and tomatoes.

3 Make a dressing with the oil and vinegar. Season with salt and black pepper. Pour it over the salad and mix well. Allow to stand in a cool place for at least 2 hours before serving, garnished with the basil.

# RAVIOLI WITH WALNUT AND CHEESE FILLING

*Ravioli con Ricotta e Noci*

H ere home-made pasta is filled with a classic combination of walnuts and cheese. It may be served on its own or with a sauce of your choice.

### INGREDIENTS
*200g/7oz/1½ cups strong plain flour*
*2.5ml/½ tsp salt*
*15ml/1 tbsp olive oil*
*2 eggs, beaten*

### FOR THE FILLING
*1 small red onion, finely chopped*
*1 small green pepper, finely chopped*
*1 carrot, coarsely grated*
*15ml/1 tbsp olive oil*
*50g/2oz/½ cup walnuts, chopped*
*115g/4oz ricotta cheese*
*30ml/2 tbsp freshly grated Parmesan or Pecorino cheese*
*15ml/1 tbsp chopped fresh marjoram*
*salt and ground black pepper*
*extra oil or melted butter, to serve*
*fresh basil sprigs, to garnish*

### SERVES 6

1 Sift the flour and salt into a food processor. With the machine running, trickle in the oil and eggs and blend to a stiff but smooth dough. Allow the machine to run for at least 1 minute if possible, otherwise remove the dough and knead by hand on a lightly floured surface for 5 minutes.

2 If using a pasta machine, break off small balls of dough and then feed them several times through the rollers.

3 If rolling by hand, divide the dough into two and roll out each piece on a lightly floured surface to a thickness of about 5mm/¼in using a rolling pin. Fold each piece of pasta into three and re-roll. Repeat this process up to six times until the dough is smooth and no longer sticky. Roll the pasta slightly more thinly each time.

4 Keep the rolled dough under clean, dry dish towels while you complete the rest and make the filling. You should aim to have an even number of pasta sheets, all the same size if rolling by machine.

5 To make the filling, fry the onion, pepper and carrot in the oil for 5 minutes, then allow to cool. Mix with the walnuts, cheeses, marjoram and seasoning.

6 Lay a pasta sheet on a lightly floured surface and place small scoops of the filling in neat rows about 5cm/2in apart. Brush in between with a little water and then place another pasta sheet on the top.

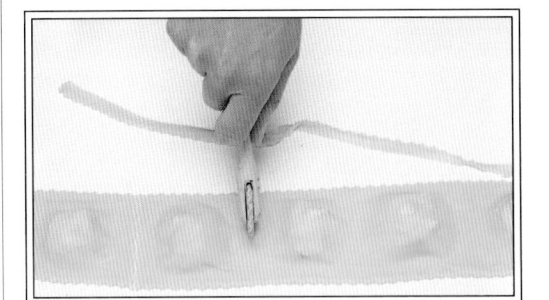

7 Press down well in between the rows then, using a ravioli or pastry cutter, cut into squares. Press the edges gently together with your fingers. Leave the ravioli in the fridge until dry, then boil in plenty of lightly salted water for just 5 minutes. Toss in a little oil or melted butter before serving, garnished with basil sprigs.

# CANNELLONI WITH CHICKEN AND MUSHROOMS
## Cannelloni con Pollo e Funghi

 lighter alternative to the usual beef-filled, béchamel-coated dish. Fill with ricotta, onion and mushroom for a vegetarian version.

### INGREDIENTS
*450g/1lb boneless, skinless chicken breast, cooked*
*225g/8oz mushrooms*
*2 garlic cloves, crushed*
*30ml/2 tbsp chopped fresh parsley*
*15ml/1 tbsp chopped fresh tarragon*
*1 egg, beaten*
*fresh lemon juice*
*12–18 cannelloni tubes*
*600ml/1 pint/2½ cups tomato sauce*
*50g/2oz/½ cup freshly grated Parmesan cheese*
*salt and ground black pepper*
*fresh parsley sprigs, to garnish*

*SERVES 4–6*

1 Preheat the oven to 200°C/400°F/Gas 6. Place the chicken in a food processor or blender and process until finely minced. Transfer to a bowl.

2 Place the mushrooms, garlic, parsley and tarragon in the food processor or blender and process until finely minced.

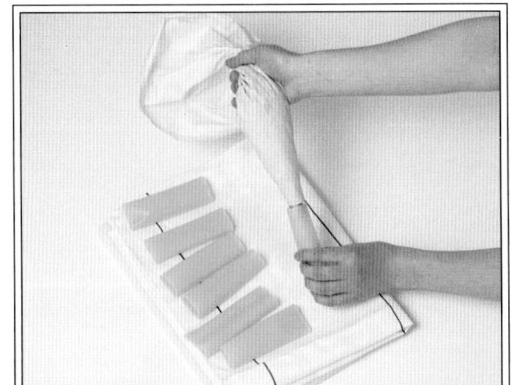

3 Beat the mushroom mixture into the minced chicken with the egg, salt and black pepper and lemon juice to taste.

4 If necessary, cook the cannelloni in plenty of salted boiling water according to the manufacturer's instructions. Drain well on a clean dish towel.

5 Place the filling in a piping bag fitted with a large plain nozzle. Use this to fill each tube of cannelloni.

6 Lay the filled cannelloni tightly together in a single layer in a buttered shallow ovenproof dish. Spoon over the tomato sauce so all the cannelloni are covered, and sprinkle evenly with the Parmesan cheese. Bake in the oven for 30 minutes or until browned and bubbling. Serve on warmed plates garnished with a parsley sprig.

# PASTA WITH TOMATOES AND ROCKET

*Pasta con Pomodori e Rucola*

**T**his pretty coloured pasta dish relies for its success on the salad green, rocket. Its delicious slightly hot, peppery taste adds a surprising touch to the final result.

### INGREDIENTS
*450g/1lb pasta shells (conchiglie)*
*450g/1lb very ripe cherry tomatoes*
*75g/3oz fresh rocket*
*45ml/3 tbsp olive oil*
*salt and ground black pepper*
*Parmesan cheese, to serve*

### SERVES 4

1 Cook the pasta in plenty of boiling salted water according to the manufacturer's instructions. Drain well.

2 Halve the tomatoes. Trim, wash and dry the rocket.

3 Heat the oil in a large saucepan, add the halved tomatoes and cook them for barely 1 minute. The tomatoes should only just heat through and not disintegrate. Remove the pan from the heat.

4 Shave the Parmesan cheese using a rotary vegetable peeler.

5 Add the pasta, then the rocket, to the tomatoes. Carefully stir to mix and heat through. Season well with salt and freshly ground black pepper. Serve immediately with plenty of shaved Parmesan cheese.

# PASTA WITH TUNA, CAPERS AND ANCHOVIES

*Pasta con Tonno, Caperi e Acciughe*

his piquant sauce is perfect for impromptu suppers – vary it according to what is in your cupboard. Add sliced peppers and garlic, or substitute canned artichoke hearts and olives for the tuna, anchovies and capers.

### INGREDIENTS
*400g/14oz canned tuna fish in oil*
*30ml/2 tbsp olive oil*
*2 garlic cloves, crushed*
*750g/1¾lb canned chopped tomatoes*
*6 canned anchovy fillets, drained*
*30ml/2 tbsp capers in vinegar, drained*
*30ml/2 tbsp chopped fresh basil*
*450g/1lb garganelle, penne*
*or rigatoni*
*salt and ground black pepper*
*fresh basil sprigs, to garnish*

### SERVES 4

1 Drain the oil from the tuna into a saucepan, add the olive oil and heat gently until it stops "spitting".

2 Add the garlic to the pan and fry over a gentle heat, stirring, until golden. Stir in the tomatoes and simmer for 25 minutes, until thickened.

3 Flake the tuna and cut the anchovies in half. Stir into the sauce *(left)* with the capers and chopped basil. Season well.

4 Cook the pasta in plenty of boiling salted water according to the manufacturer's instructions. Drain well and toss with the sauce. Garnish with fresh basil sprigs.

# BAKED LASAGNE
## *Lasagne al Forno*

his is the classic lasagne – rich meat sauce and lightly spiced béchamel layered with pasta sheets and Parmesan cheese.

### INGREDIENTS
*450g/1lb no pre-cook lasagne*
*115g/4oz/1 cup grated Parmesan cheese*
*25g/1oz butter*

### FOR THE BOLOGNESE SAUCE
*60ml/4 tbsp olive oil*
*1 onion, finely chopped*
*2 streaky bacon rashers, chopped*
*1 carrot, finely chopped*
*1 celery stalk, finely chopped*
*1 garlic clove, crushed*
*350g/12oz minced beef*
*350ml/12fl oz/1½ cups red wine*
*400g/14oz can chopped tomatoes*
*1 bay leaf*

### FOR THE BECHAMEL SAUCE
*750ml/1¼ pints/3⅔ cups milk*
*1 bay leaf*
*3 mace blades*
*115g/4oz/½ cup butter*
*75g/3oz/¾ cup plain flour*
*salt and ground black pepper*

*SERVES 8–10*

1 First make the Bolognese sauce, heat the oil in a heavy saucepan, add the onion and cook over a gentle heat for 5 minutes. Add the bacon, carrot, celery and garlic and cook for 2–3 minutes more.

2 Stir in the minced beef and cook until browned. Add the wine, tomatoes and bay leaf and season to taste. Bring to the boil, then reduce the heat and simmer gently for 45 minutes.

3 Meanwhile, make the béchamel sauce. Heat the milk with the bay leaf and mace until almost boiling, then leave to stand for 15 minutes. Melt the butter in a pan, stir in the flour and cook for 1 minute. Strain in the milk, whisking all the time, bring to the boil, still whisking, and cook until thickened. Season to taste.

### VARIATION
Reduce the amount of beef in the Bolognese sauce by 115g/4oz and add 115g/4oz sliced mushrooms with the wine and tomatoes instead.

4 Preheat the oven to 200°C/400°F/Gas 6. Spread a little Bolognese sauce in an ovenproof dish. Arrange two or three sheets of lasagne on top, cover with Bolognese sauce and then béchamel, then sprinkle with a little of the Parmesan.

5 Repeat the layers, ending with a layer of béchamel sauce. Sprinkle with Parmesan and dot with butter. Bake for 20–30 minutes until well browned and bubbling. Leave to stand for 5 minutes, then serve hot.

# TAGLIATELLE WITH GORGONZOLA

*Tagliatelle con la Gorgonzola*

Gorgonzola is a mild creamy blue-veined cheese from Lombardy in northern Italy. As an alternative you could use Danish blue.

INGREDIENTS

*25g/1oz/2 tbsp butter, plus extra for tossing the pasta*
*225g/8oz Gorgonzola cheese, crumbled*
*150ml/¼ pint/⅔ cup double or whipping cream*
*30ml/2 tbsp dry vermouth*
*5ml/1 tsp cornflour*
*15ml/1 tbsp chopped fresh sage*
*450g/1lb tagliatelle*
*salt and ground black pepper*

*SERVES 4*

1 Melt the butter in a heavy-based saucepan. Stir in 175g/6oz of the crumbled Gorgonzola cheese and cook, stirring over a very gentle heat for 2–3 minutes until the cheese is melted.

2 Pour in the cream, vermouth and cornflour, whisking well to amalgamate. Stir in the chopped sage, then taste for seasoning. Cook, whisking all the time, until the sauce boils and thickens. Set aside.

3 Cook the tagliatelle in plenty of boiling, salted water for about 10 minutes. Drain thoroughly and toss with a little butter.

4 Reheat the sauce gently, whisking well *(right)*. Divide the pasta among four warmed serving bowls, top with the sauce and sprinkle over the remaining cheese. Serve immediately.

# FETTUCCINE WITH PARMESAN AND CREAM
*Fettuccine all'Alfredo*

classic dish from Rome, Fettuccine all'Alfredo is simply pasta tossed with double cream, butter, nutmeg and freshly grated Parmesan cheese. Popular but less traditional additions are tiny green peas and thin strips of ham.

### INGREDIENTS
*25g/1oz/2 tbsp butter*
*150ml/¼ pint/⅔ cup double cream, plus*
*60ml/4 tbsp extra*
*450g/1lb fettuccine*
*50g/2oz/½ cup freshly grated Parmesan*
*cheese, plus extra to serve*
*freshly grated nutmeg*
*salt and ground black pepper*
*dill sprigs, to garnish*

### SERVES 4

1 Place the butter and double cream in a heavy-based saucepan, bring to the boil and simmer for 1 minute until the mixture is slightly thickened. Remove the pan from the heat and set aside.

2 Cook the fettuccine in plenty of boiling salted water according to the manufacturer's instructions, but for 2 minutes less than the time stated. The pasta should still be a little firm.

3 Drain the pasta thoroughly and transfer to the pan with the cream sauce.

4 Return the pan to the heat and turn the pasta in the sauce to coat.

5 Add the remaining 4 tablespoons of double cream, the grated Parmesan cheese, salt and pepper to taste, and a little grated nutmeg. Toss until the pasta is thoroughly coated with the sauce and heated right through. Serve immediately from the pan and top with extra grated Parmesan cheese. Garnish with dill sprigs.

# PASTA WITH TOMATO SAUCE

*Pasta Napoletana*

his classic cooked tomato sauce is simplicity itself – it goes well with almost any pasta shape.

## INGREDIENTS

*450g/1lb pasta, any variety*
*freshly grated Parmesan cheese, to serve*

### FOR THE TOMATO SAUCE

*900g/2lb fresh ripe red tomatoes or*
*750g/1¾lb canned plum tomatoes*
*with juice*
*1 onion, chopped*
*1 carrot, diced*
*1 celery stick, diced*
*150ml/¼ pint/⅔ cup dry white*
*wine (optional)*
*1 fresh parsley sprig*
*pinch of sugar*
*15ml/1 tbsp chopped fresh oregano*
*salt and ground black pepper*
*fresh basil sprigs, to garnish*

SERVES 4

---

### COOK'S TIP

To stop pasta from sticking together while it is boiling, add a little oil to the cooking water first.

---

1 To make the tomato sauce, roughly chop the tomatoes, remove the cores, then place the tomatoes in a large saucepan.

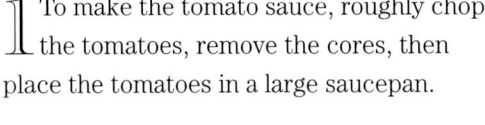

2 Put all the remaining sauce ingredients, except the oregano, into the pan with the tomatoes, bring to the boil and simmer, half-covered, for 45 minutes until very thick, stirring occasionally. Pass through a sieve, or liquidize, then pour through a sieve to remove the tomato seeds. Stir in the chopped oregano. Taste for seasoning.

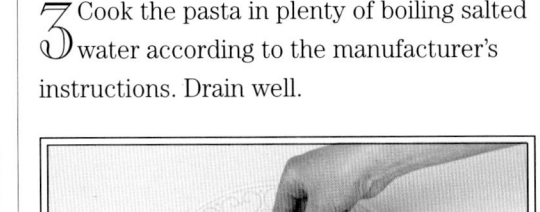

3 Cook the pasta in plenty of boiling salted water according to the manufacturer's instructions. Drain well.

4 Toss the pasta with the sauce. Serve with Parmesan, garnished with basil.

# SEAFOOD PIZZA

*Pizza con Frutti di Mare*

ny combination of shellfish or other seafood can be used as a pizza topping. Aim for an interesting combination of flavours and textures.

### INGREDIENTS
*450g/1lb peeled plum tomatoes, fresh or canned, weighed whole, without extra juice*
*175g/6oz small squid*
*225g/8oz fresh mussels*
*1 quantity Pizza Dough (see page 39)*
*175g/6oz prawns, raw or cooked, peeled and deveined*
*2 garlic cloves, finely chopped*
*45ml/3 tbsp chopped fresh parsley*
*45ml/3 tbsp olive oil*
*salt and ground black pepper*

*SERVES 4*

---

### VARIATION
Fresh clams may be added: scrub well under cold running water. Heat in a saucepan until the shells open. Lift out and remove to a dish. Discard any that do not open. Break off the empty half shells, and discard. Add to the pizza after 8 minutes of baking.

---

1 Preheat the oven to 240°C/475°F/Gas 9 at least 20 minutes before baking the pizza. Strain the tomatoes through the medium holes of a food mill placed over a bowl, scraping in all the pulp.

2 Working near the sink, clean the squid by first peeling off the thin skin from the body section. Rinse thoroughly. Pull the head and tentacles away from the body section. Some of the intestines will come away with the head.

3 Remove and discard the translucent quill and any remaining insides from the body. Sever the tentacles from the head. Discard the head and intestines. Remove the small hard beak from the base of the tentacles. Rinse the body and tentacles under running water. Drain. Slice the bodies into 5mm/¼in rings. Pat dry with kitchen paper.

4 Scrape any barnacles off the mussels, and scrub well with a stiff brush. Rinse in several changes of cold water. Place the mussels in a saucepan and heat until they open. Lift them out with a slotted spoon, and remove to a side dish. (Discard any that do not open.) Break off the empty half shells, and discard.

5 Roll out the dough to a 25cm/10in round. Spread some of the puréed tomatoes on it, leaving the rim uncovered. Dot with the prawns, squid rings and tentacles. Sprinkle with the garlic, parsley, salt and pepper, and olive oil. Immediately place the pizza in the oven. Bake for about 8 minutes.

6 Remove from the oven, and add the mussels in the half shells. Return to the oven and bake for a further 7–10 minutes, or until the crust is golden.

# CALZONE
*Calzone*

alzone are simply pizzas with the topping on the inside. This vegetable filling is delicious but you could change the ingredients if you like.

INGREDIENTS
FOR THE PIZZA DOUGH
*450g/1lb/4 cups plain flour*
*1 sachet easy-blend dried yeast*
*about 350ml/12fl oz/1½ cups warm water*

FOR THE FILLING
*5ml/1 tsp olive oil*
*1 red onion, thinly sliced*
*3 courgettes, sliced*
*2 large tomatoes, diced*
*150g/5oz mozzarella, diced*
*15ml/1 tbsp chopped fresh oregano*
*skimmed milk, to glaze*
*salt and ground black pepper*
*fresh oregano sprigs, to garnish*

*MAKES 4*

COOK'S TIP
Don't add too much water to the dough
when mixing otherwise it will be
difficult to roll out – the dough should
be soft, but not at all sticky.

1 To make the dough, sift the flour and a pinch of salt into a bowl and stir in the yeast. Stir in just enough warm water to mix to a soft but not sticky dough.

2 Knead for 5 minutes until smooth. Cover with clear film or a dish towel and leave in a warm place for about 1 hour, or until doubled in size.

3 Meanwhile, make the filling. Heat the oil and sauté the onion and courgettes for 3–4 minutes. Remove from the heat and add the tomatoes, mozzarella and oregano and season to taste with salt and pepper. Preheat the oven to 220°C/425°F/Gas 7 for at least 20 minutes.

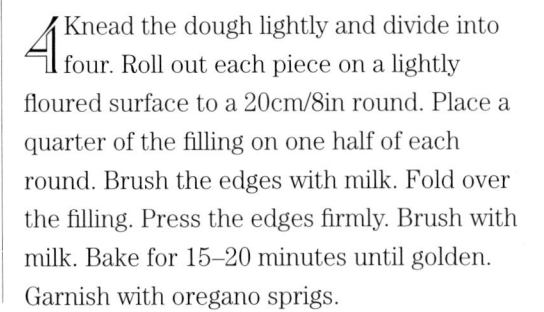

4 Knead the dough lightly and divide into four. Roll out each piece on a lightly floured surface to a 20cm/8in round. Place a quarter of the filling on one half of each round. Brush the edges with milk. Fold over the filling. Press the edges firmly. Brush with milk. Bake for 15–20 minutes until golden. Garnish with oregano sprigs.

# PEPPERONI PIZZA

*Pizza con Salame*

 weet peppers, pepperoni and black olives make a glorious topping for this classic pizza.

### INGREDIENTS

### FOR THE SAUCE

*30ml/2 tbsp olive oil*
*1 onion, finely chopped*
*1 garlic clove, crushed*
*400g/14oz can chopped tomatoes*
*15ml/1 tbsp tomato purée*

### FOR THE PIZZA DOUGH

*275g/10oz/2½ cups plain flour*
*2.5ml/½ tsp salt*
*5ml/1 tsp easy-blend dried yeast*
*about 175ml/6fl oz/¾ cup warm water*
*30ml/2 tbsp olive oil*

### FOR THE TOPPING

*½ each red, yellow and green pepper,*
*sliced into rings*
*150g/5oz mozzarella, sliced*
*75g/3oz/½ cup thinly sliced pepperoni*
*8 black olives, stoned*
*3 sun-dried tomatoes in oil, chopped*
*2.5ml/½ tsp dried oregano*
*olive oil, for drizzling*
*fresh basil sprigs, to garnish*

*SERVES 4*

1 To make the sauce, heat the oil in a pan, add the onion and garlic and fry gently for about 6 minutes. Stir in the tomatoes and the tomato purée. Bring to the boil and boil rapidly for 5 minutes. Remove from the heat and leave to cool.

2 For the pizza base, lightly grease a 30cm/12in round pizza tray. Sift the flour and salt into a bowl. Sprinkle over the yeast and make a well in the centre. Pour in the water and olive oil. Mix to a soft dough.

3 Knead the dough for 5–10 minutes, until smooth. Roll out to a 25cm/10in round, making the edges slightly thicker than the centre. Lift on to the pizza tray.

4 Preheat the oven to 220°C/425°F/Gas 7. Spread the sauce over the dough. Add the topping ingredients. Drizzle with oil. Cover loosely and leave in a warm place for 30 minutes.

5 Bake for 25–30 minutes and serve hot, garnished with a basil sprig.

# PUMPKIN AND PISTACHIO RISOTTO

*Risotto con Zucca e Pistacchi*

 his elegant combination of creamy golden rice and orange pumpkin can be made as pale or bright as you like by adding different quantities of saffron.

### INGREDIENTS

*1.2 litres/2 pints/5 cups vegetable stock*
*or water*
*generous pinch of saffron threads*
*30ml/2 tbsp olive oil*
*1 onion, chopped*
*2 garlic cloves, crushed*
*450g/1lb arborio rice*
*900g/2lb pumpkin, peeled, seeded and*
*cut into 2cm/³⁄₄in cubes*
*175ml/6fl oz/³⁄₄ cup dry white wine*
*15g/¹⁄₂oz Parmesan cheese, finely grated*
*50g/2oz/¹⁄₂ cup pistachios*
*45ml/3 tbsp chopped fresh marjoram or*
*oregano, plus extra leaves, to garnish*
*freshly grated nutmeg*
*salt and ground black pepper*

*SERVES 4*

---

### COOK'S TIP
Italian arborio rice must be used for a true risotto. Choose unpolished white arborio as it contains more starch.

---

1 Bring the stock or water to the boil, then reduce to a low simmer. Ladle a little stock into a small bowl. Add the saffron threads and leave to infuse.

2 Heat the oil in a large saucepan. Add the onion and garlic and cook gently for about 5 minutes until softened. Add the rice and pumpkin and cook for a few minutes longer until the rice looks transparent.

3 Pour in the wine and allow it to bubble fiercely. When the wine is absorbed add about a quarter of the stock and the infused saffron liquid. Stir constantly until all the liquid is absorbed.

4 Gradually add the remaining stock or water, a ladleful at a time, allowing the rice to absorb all the liquid before adding more, and stirring all the time. After 20–30 minutes the rice should be golden yellow and creamy, and *al dente* when tested.

5 Remove the pan from the heat and stir in the Parmesan cheese. Cover the pan and leave the risotto to stand for 5 minutes.

6 To finish the risotto, stir in the pistachios and chopped marjoram or oregano. Season to taste with a little nutmeg, salt and pepper, and scatter over a few extra marjoram or oregano leaves as a garnish, before serving.

# GRILLED POLENTA WITH GORGONZOLA

## *Polenta alla Griglia*

G rilled polenta is delicious, and is a good way of using up cold polenta. Try it with any soft flavourful cheese. Plain grilled polenta is also a good accompaniment to stews and soups.

### INGREDIENTS

*1.5 litres/2½ pints/6¼ cups water*

*15ml/1 tbsp salt*

*350g/12oz/2½ cups polenta flour*

*225g/8oz/1¼ cups Gorgonzola or other cheese, at room temperature*

*SERVES 6–8 AS A SNACK OR APPETIZER*

1 Bring the water to the boil in a large heavy-based saucepan, and add the salt. Reduce the heat to a simmer, and gradually add the polenta flour in a fine rain. Stir constantly with a whisk until all the polenta has been added.

2 Switch to a long-handled wooden spoon, and continue to stir the polenta over a low to moderate heat until it is a thick mass, and pulls away from the sides of the pan. This may take from around 25–50 minutes, depending on the type of flour used. For best results, never stop stirring the polenta until you remove it from the heat.

3 When the polenta is cooked, sprinkle a work surface or large board with a little water. Spread the polenta out onto the surface in a layer approximately 1.5cm/¾in in thickness. Allow to cool completely. Preheat the grill.

4 Cut the polenta into triangles. Grill the pieces until hot and speckled with brown on both sides. Spread with the Gorgonzola or other cheese. Serve immediately as a starter, a snack or as an accompaniment.

# POTATO AND RED PEPPER FRITTATA

*Frittata di Patate*

Fresh herbs make all the difference in this simple but delicious recipe – fresh parsley or chives could be substituted for the chopped mint.

INGREDIENTS
*450g/1lb small new potatoes*
*6 eggs*
*30ml/2 tbsp chopped fresh mint*
*30ml/2 tbsp olive oil*
*1 onion, chopped*
*2 garlic cloves, crushed*
*2 red peppers, seeded and roughly chopped*
*salt and ground black pepper*
*mint sprigs, to garnish*

SERVES 3–4

1 Cook the potatoes in boiling salted water until just tender. Drain, leave to cool slightly, then cut into thick slices.

2 Whisk together the eggs, mint and seasoning in a bowl, then set aside. Heat the oil in a large frying pan.

3 Add the onion, garlic, peppers and potatoes to the pan and cook, stirring, for 5 minutes.

4 Pour the egg mixture over the vegetables and stir gently. Push the mixture into the centre of the pan *(left)* as it cooks to allow the liquid egg to run on to the base. Turn the heat to low.

5 Once the egg mixture is lightly set, place the pan under a hot grill for 2–3 minutes, until golden brown. Serve the frittata hot or cold, cut into wedges and garnished with mint sprigs.

# SPINACH GNOCCHI

*Gnocchi di Spinaci*

his wholesome dish is ideal for making in advance then baking when required. Serve it with a fresh tomato sauce.

### INGREDIENTS
*400g/14oz fresh leaf spinach or 175g/6oz*
*frozen leaf spinach, thawed*
*750ml/1¼ pints/3 cups milk*
*200g/7oz/1¼ cups semolina*
*50g/2oz/4 tbsp butter, melted*
*50g/2oz Parmesan cheese, freshly grated,*
*plus extra to serve*
*freshly grated nutmeg*
*2 eggs, beaten*
*salt and ground black pepper*

*SERVES 4–6*

---

#### VARIATION
For a more substantial meal, make a tasty vegetable base of lightly sautéed peppers, courgettes and mushrooms. Place the gnocchi on top.

---

1 Blanch the spinach in the tiniest amount of water then drain and squeeze dry through a sieve with the back of a ladle. Chop the spinach roughly.

2 In a large saucepan, heat the milk and, when just on the point of boiling, sprinkle in the semolina in a steady stream, stirring it briskly with a wooden spoon.

3 Simmer the semolina for 2 minutes, then remove from the heat and stir in half of the butter, most of the cheese, the nutmeg and spinach, and season to taste with salt and pepper. Allow to cool for 5 minutes.

4 Stir in the eggs, then tip the mixture out on to a shallow baking sheet, spreading it to a 1cm/½in thickness. Allow to cool completely, then chill until the texture is quite solid.

5 Stamp out shapes from the prepared gnocchi mixture using a 4cm/1½in plain round pastry cutter. Put the trimmings on a plate and reserve.

6 Grease a shallow ovenproof dish. Place the trimmings on the base and arrange the gnocchi rounds on top with each one overlapping. Brush the tops with the remaining butter and sprinkle over the remaining cheese.

7 When you are ready to bake, preheat the oven to 190°C/375°F/Gas 5 and cook the gnocchi for about 35 minutes until golden and crisp on top. Serve hot with fresh tomato sauce and hand round a small bowl of freshly grated Parmesan cheese.

# BAKED FENNEL
## *Finocchio Gratinato*

ennel is widely eaten all over Italy, both in its raw and cooked form. It is delicious married with the sharpness of Parmesan cheese in this dish.

### INGREDIENTS
*1kg/2¼lb fennel bulbs, washed and halved*
*50g/2oz/4 tbsp butter*
*40g/1½oz/⅓ cup freshly grated Parmesan cheese*

### SERVES 4–6

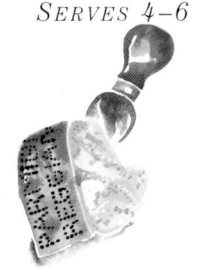

---

### VARIATION
For a more substantial version of this dish, scatter 75g/3oz chopped ham, bacon or pancetta over the fennel before topping with the grated Parmesan cheese.

1 Preheat the oven to 200°C/400°F/Gas 6. Cook the fennel in a large pan of boiling water until soft but not mushy. Drain.

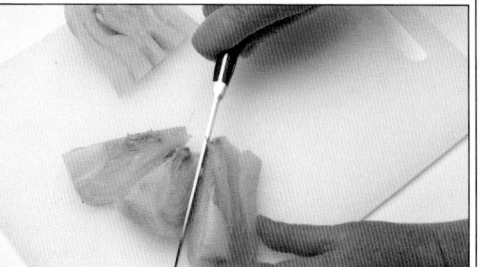

2 Cut the fennel bulbs lengthways into four or six pieces. Place them in a buttered baking dish.

3 Dot with butter, then sprinkle with the grated Parmesan. Bake for 20 minutes until golden brown. Serve at once.

# AUBERGINE BAKED WITH CHEESE

*Parmigiana di Melanzane*

his famous dish is a speciality of Italy's southern regions. In Campania, around Naples, slices of hard-boiled egg are sometimes added with the mozzarella.

INGREDIENTS

*1kg/2¼lb aubergines*
*flour, for coating*
*oil, for frying*
*40g/1½oz/⅓ cup freshly grated*
*Parmesan cheese*
*400g/14oz/2 cups mozzarella, sliced*
*very thinly*
*salt and ground black pepper*

FOR THE TOMATO SAUCE
*60ml/4 tbsp olive oil*
*1 onion, very finely chopped*
*1 garlic clove, finely chopped*
*450g/1lb tomatoes, fresh or canned,*
*chopped, with their juice*
*a few fresh basil leaves or parsley sprigs*
*salt and ground black pepper*

SERVES 4–6

1 Cut the aubergines into rounds about 1cm/½in thick, sprinkle with salt, and leave to drain for about 1 hour.

2 Meanwhile make the tomato sauce. Heat the oil in a saucepan. Add the onion and cook over a moderate heat for 5–8 minutes until translucent. Stir in the garlic and the tomatoes (add 45ml/3 tbsp water if using fresh tomatoes). Add the herbs and season. Cook for 20–30 minutes. Purée in a blender.

3 Pat the aubergine slices dry with kitchen paper. Coat lightly in flour. Heat a little oil in a large frying pan. Add one layer of aubergine, and cook, covered, over a low heat, turning once, until soft. Repeat with the remaining slices.

4 Preheat the oven to 180°C/350°F/Gas 4. Grease a wide shallow baking dish. Pour a little tomato sauce in the base. Cover with a layer of aubergine. Sprinkle with a little Parmesan, season and cover with a layer of mozzarella and some sauce. Repeat, finishing with tomato sauce and a sprinkling of Parmesan. Sprinkle with a little olive oil, and bake for 45 minutes.

# GRILLED SARDINES
### *Sarde alla Griglia*

resh sardines are flavourful and firm-fleshed, and quite different in taste and consistency from those canned in oil. They are excellent plainly grilled and served with lemon.

### INGREDIENTS
*1kg/2lb fresh sardines, gutted and with heads removed*
*olive oil, for brushing*
*salt and ground black pepper*
*45ml/3 tbsp chopped fresh parsley and lemon wedges, to garnish*

### SERVES 4–6

1 Preheat the grill. Rinse the sardines inside and out with cold running water. Pat dry thoroughly with kitchen paper.

2 Brush the sardines lightly with olive oil *(left)* and sprinkle generously with salt and pepper. Place the sardines in a single layer on the grill pan. Grill for 3–4 minutes.

3 Turn, and cook for 3–4 minutes more, or until the skins begin to brown. Serve immediately, garnished with the chopped parsley and lemon wedges.

# SPAGHETTI WITH MUSSELS

*Spaghetti con le Cozze*

ussels are popular in all the coastal regions of Italy, and are delicious with pasta. If you like, reserve a few in their half-shells for decoration.

### INGREDIENTS

*1kg/2¼lb fresh mussels, in their shells*
*400g/14oz spaghetti*
*75ml/5 tbsp olive oil*
*3 garlic cloves, finely chopped*
*60ml/4 tbsp chopped fresh parsley*
*60ml/4 tbsp white wine*
*salt and ground black pepper*

*SERVES 4*

1 Scrub the mussels well under cold running water, pulling off the "beard" with a small sharp knife.

2 Bring a large pan of water to the boil for the pasta. Place the mussels with a cupful of water in another large saucepan over a moderate heat. As soon as they open, lift them out one by one.

3 When all the mussels have opened (discard any that do not), strain the liquid in the saucepan through a layer of kitchen paper into a bowl and set aside until needed. Add salt to the pan of boiling water, and add the spaghetti.

4 Meanwhile, heat the oil in large frying pan. Add the garlic and parsley, and cook for 2–3 minutes. Add the mussels, the reserved juice and the wine and simmer very gently. Add a generous amount of freshly ground black pepper, then taste for seasoning and add salt, if necessary.

5 Drain the spaghetti when it is *al dente*. Tip it into the frying pan with the sauce, and stir well over a moderate heat for a few minutes more, then serve at once.

# TUNA WITH PAN-FRIED TOMATOES

## *Tonno con Pomodori Fritti*

 una steaks served with a fresh, piquant sauce make a wonderful and easy-to-prepare supper dish.

### INGREDIENTS

*2 tuna steaks, about 175g/6oz each*
*90ml/6 tbsp olive oil*
*30ml/2 tbsp lemon juice*
*2 garlic cloves, chopped*
*5ml/1 tsp chopped fresh thyme*
*4 canned anchovy fillets, drained and finely chopped*
*225g/8oz plum tomatoes, halved*
*30ml/2 tbsp chopped fresh parsley*
*4–6 black olives, stoned and chopped*
*ground black pepper*
*crusty bread, to serve*

### SERVES 2

### COOK'S TIP

If you are unable to find fresh tuna steaks, you could replace them with salmon fillets, if you like – just cook them for 1–2 minutes more on each side.

1 Place the tuna steaks in a shallow non-metallic dish. Mix 60ml/4 tbsp of the oil with the lemon juice, garlic, thyme, anchovies and pepper. Pour this mixture over the tuna and leave to marinate for at least 1 hour.

2 Lift the tuna from the marinade and place on a grill rack. Grill for 4 minutes on each side, or until the tuna feels firm to the touch, basting with some of the marinade. Take care not to overcook.

3 Meanwhile, heat the remaining oil in a frying pan. Add the tomatoes and fry for just 2 minutes on each side.

4 Divide the tomatoes equally between two warmed serving plates and scatter over the chopped parsley and olives. Place the tuna steaks on top of the tomatoes.

5 Add the remaining marinade to the pan juices and warm through. Pour over the tomatoes and tuna steaks and serve at once with crusty bread for mopping up the juices.

# MILANESE VEAL
*Ossobuco alla Milanese*

O ssobuco means "hollow bone", and this dish calls for shin of veal cut into sections across the bone. Each bone should have its centre of marrow, which is considered a great delicacy.

INGREDIENTS

*50g/2oz/4 tbsp butter*
*1 garlic clove, crushed*
*4 pieces shin of veal, each about 5cm/2in thick*
*flour for dredging*
*250ml/8fl oz/1 cup dry white wine*
*300ml/½ pint/1¼ cups meat or chicken stock*
*1 bay leaf*
*1 sprig fresh thyme, or ¼ tsp dried thyme*
*salt and ground black pepper*

FOR THE GREMOLATA

*1 small garlic clove*
*30ml/2 tbsp chopped fresh parsley*
*5ml/1 tsp chopped lemon rind*
*½ anchovy fillet (optional)*

*SERVES 4*

1 Preheat the oven to 160°C/325°F/Gas 3. Heat the butter with the crushed garlic clove in a heavy casserole large enough for the meat to fit in one layer.

2 Dredge the veal lightly in flour. Add to the pan and brown on both sides. Season with salt and pepper.

3 Add the wine, and cook over a moderate heat for 3–4 minutes, turning the veal several times. Add the stock, bay leaf and thyme. Cover, and bake for 2 hours.

4 Meanwhile, prepare the gremolata by combining the garlic, parsley, lemon rind and anchovy, if using, on a board and chopping them very finely.

5 Remove the casserole from the oven. Taste the sauce for seasoning. Add the gremolata, and mix it well into the sauce. Return the casserole to the oven for a further 10 minutes, then serve.

# PORK WITH GREMOLATA

*Maiale con la Gremolata*

he ever-popular gremolata dressing adds a hint of sharpness to this pork dish. This version gains extra subtlety by using lime rind as well as lemon.

INGREDIENTS

*30ml/2 tbsp olive oil*
*4 pork shoulder steaks, about*
*175g/6oz each*
*1 onion, chopped*
*2 garlic cloves, crushed*
*30ml/2 tbsp tomato purée*
*400g/14oz can chopped tomatoes*
*150ml/¼ pint/⅔ cup dry white wine*
*bunch of mixed fresh herbs*
*3 anchovy fillets, drained and chopped*
*salt and ground black pepper*
*salad, to serve*

FOR THE GREMOLATA
*45ml/3 tbsp chopped fresh parsley*
*grated rind of ½ lemon*
*grated rind of 1 lime*
*1 garlic clove, chopped*

*SERVES 4*

1 Heat the oil in a large flameproof casserole, add the pork steaks and brown on both sides. Remove the steaks.

2 Add the onion to the casserole and cook until soft and beginning to brown. Add the garlic and cook for 1–2 minutes, then stir in the tomato purée, chopped tomatoes and wine. Add the bunch of mixed herbs. Bring to the boil, then boil rapidly for 3–4 minutes to reduce and thicken slightly.

3 Return the pork to the casserole, then cover and cook for about 30 minutes. Stir in the chopped anchovies.

4 Cover and cook for 15 minutes, or until the pork is tender. Meanwhile, to make the gremolata, combine the parsley, lemon and lime rinds and garlic.

5 Remove the pork steaks and discard the bunch of herbs. Reduce the sauce over a high heat, if it is not already thick. Taste and adjust the seasoning.

6 Return the pork to the casserole, then sprinkle with the gremolata. Cover and cook for 5 minutes. Serve hot with a salad.

# ROAST LAMB WITH HERBS AND GARLIC

*Arrosto d'Agnello con Erbe e Aglio*

T his dish originates from southern Italy, where lamb is simply roasted spiked with slivers of garlic and wild herbs from the mountains.

INGREDIENTS

*1.5kg/3–3½lb leg of lamb*
*45–60ml/3–4 tbsp olive oil*
*4 garlic cloves, halved*
*2 sprigs fresh sage, or pinch of dried sage*
*2 sprigs fresh rosemary, or 5ml/1 tsp dried rosemary*
*2 bay leaves*
*2 sprigs fresh thyme, or 2.5ml/½ tsp dried thyme*
*175ml/6fl oz/¾ cup dry white wine*
*salt and ground black pepper*
*fresh herbs, to garnish*

*SERVES 4–6*

**1** Trim any excess fat from the lamb. Rub with olive oil. Make small cuts in the skin all over the meat. Insert the garlic in some and a few of the fresh herbs in the others. (If using dried herbs, sprinkle on the meat.)

**2** Place the remaining fresh herbs on the lamb, and allow it to stand in a cool place for at least 2 hours before cooking. Preheat the oven to 190°C/375°F/Gas 5.

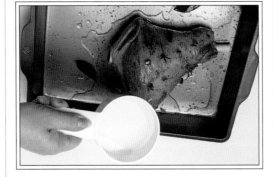

**3** Place the lamb in a large roasting tin, surrounded by the herbs. Pour on about 30ml/2 tbsp of the oil and season. Roast for 35 minutes, basting occasionally.

**4** Pour the wine over the lamb. Roast for 15 minutes, or until cooked. Put the lamb on a heated serving dish. Tilt the tin, spooning off any fat on the surface. Strain the pan juices into a gravy boat. Slice the meat, and serve the pan juices separately, as a sauce. Garnish with fresh herbs.

MEAT AND POULTRY

# CHICKEN IN PIZZAIOLA SAUCE

*Pollo alla Pizzaiola*

SERVES 4

T he combination of sweet red pepper and sun-dried tomatoes in this dish creates a wonderful, colourful sauce for the chicken.

**INGREDIENTS**

30ml/2 tbsp plain flour
4 chicken portions (legs, breasts or quarters)
30ml/2 tbsp olive oil
1 onion, chopped
2 garlic cloves, chopped
1 red pepper, seeded and chopped
400g/14oz can chopped tomatoes
30ml/2 tbsp red pesto sauce
4 sun-dried tomatoes in oil, chopped
150ml/¼ pint/⅔ cup chicken stock
5ml/1 tsp dried oregano
8 black olives, stoned
salt and ground black pepper
fresh basil sprigs, to garnish
tagliatelle, to serve

1 Put the flour in a polythene bag and season. Add the chicken and coat well. Heat the oil in a flameproof casserole, and brown the chicken, then remove.

2 Lower the heat, add the onion, garlic and pepper and cook for 5 minutes. Stir in all the remaining ingredients except the olives and bring to the boil.

3 Return the browned chicken portions to the casserole, season lightly, cover and simmer for 30–35 minutes, or until the chicken is cooked.

4 Add the olives and simmer for a further 5 minutes. Transfer to a warmed serving dish, and garnish with the fresh basil sprigs. Serve hot with tagliatelle.

# CHICKEN WITH OLIVES

*Pollo con le Olive*

[L] This tasty dish makes a good light main course and can be put together quickly for unexpected guests. It is equally good with turkey pieces.

INGREDIENTS

90ml/6 tbsp olive oil
1 garlic clove, crushed
1 dried chilli, lightly crushed
500g/1¼lb boneless chicken breast, cut into 5mm/¼in slices
120ml/4fl oz/½ cup dry white wine
4 tomatoes, peeled and seeded, cut into thin strips
24 black olives
6–8 fresh basil leaves, torn into pieces, and basil sprigs, to garnish
salt and ground black pepper

*SERVES 4*

1 Heat 60ml/4 tbsp of the olive oil in a large frying pan. Add the garlic and dried chilli, and cook over a low heat until the garlic is golden.

2 Raise the heat to moderate. Place the chicken in the pan, and brown all over for about 2 minutes. Season.

3 Remove the garlic and chilli and discard. Add the wine, tomato strips and olives, then cook over a moderate heat for 3–4 minutes. Using a wooden spoon, scrape up any meat residue from the base of the pan.

4 Return the chicken to the pan. Sprinkle with the basil leaves. Heat for about 30 seconds, to make sure it is warmed through, then serve, garnished with basil sprigs.

# CHOCOLATE AMARETTI PEACHES

*Pesche con Amaretti e Cioccolato*

uick and easy to prepare, this delicious dessert can also be made with fresh nectarines, a variety of peach with a smooth skin like a plum.

INGREDIENTS

115g/4oz amaretti biscuits, crushed
50g/2oz plain chocolate, chopped
grated rind of 1/2 orange
15ml/1 tbsp clear honey
1.5ml/1/4 tsp ground cinnamon
1 egg white, lightly beaten
4 firm ripe peaches
150ml/1/4 pint/2/3 cup white wine
15ml/1 tbsp caster sugar
whipped cream, to serve

*SERVES 4*

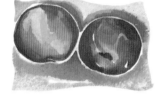

VARIATION

Omit the chocolate and increase the amaretti. Let the peaches cool, then serve on a bed of vanilla ice cream, accompanied by a raspberry sauce.

1 Preheat the oven to 190°C/375°F/Gas 5. Mix together the crushed amaretti biscuits, chocolate, orange rind, honey and cinnamon in a bowl. Add the beaten egg white and stir to bind the mixture.

2 Halve and stone the peaches and fill the cavities with the amaretti mixture, mounding it up slightly.

3 Arrange the stuffed peaches in a lightly buttered, shallow ovenproof dish which will just hold them comfortably. Pour the white wine into a measuring jug, then stir in the sugar.

4 Pour the wine mixture around the peaches. Bake for 30-40 minutes, until the peaches are tender. Spoon a little of the cooking juices over the peaches and serve with whipped cream.

# COFFEE DESSERT

*Tiramisù*

# ZABAGLIONE

*Zabaione*

**T**iramisù means "pick me up", and this rich egg and coffee dessert does just that! If you prefer, top with a sprinkling of grated chocolate instead of cocoa powder.

### INGREDIENTS
*500g/1¼lb mascarpone cheese*
*5 eggs, separated, at room temperature*
*90g/3½oz/½ cup caster sugar*
*pinch of salt*
*savoyard or sponge biscuits, to line dish(es)*
*120ml/4fl oz/½ cup strong espresso coffee*
*60ml/4 tbsp brandy or rum (optional)*
*unsweetened cocoa powder, to sprinkle*

### SERVES 6–8

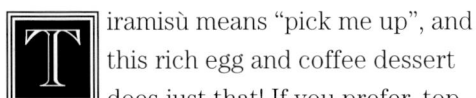

**1** Beat the mascarpone in a small bowl until soft. In a separate bowl beat the egg yolks with the sugar (reserving 15ml/1 tbsp) until the mixture is pale yellow and fluffy. Gradually beat in the softened mascarpone.

**2** Using an electric beater or wire whisk, beat the egg whites with the salt until they form stiff peaks. Fold the egg whites into the mascarpone mixture.

**3** Line one large or several individual dishes with a layer of biscuits. Pour the coffee into a measuring jug, add the reserved sugar, and stir in the brandy or rum, if using.

**4** Sprinkle the coffee over the biscuits. They should be moist but not saturated. Cover with half the egg mixture. Make another layer of biscuits moistened with coffee, and cover with the remaining egg mixture. Sprinkle with cocoa powder. Cover, and chill in the fridge for at least 1 hour, preferably more, before serving.

**T**his airy egg custard fortified with sweet wine is usually eaten warm with biscuits or fruit. A small teaspoon of ground cinnamon may be added.

### INGREDIENTS
*3 egg yolks*
*45ml/3 tbsp caster sugar*
*75ml/5 tbsp marsala or white dessert wine*
*pinch of grated orange rind*

### SERVES 3–4

**1** In the top half of a double boiler or in a bowl, away from the heat, whisk the egg yolks with the sugar until pale yellow. Beat in the marsala or wine.

**2** Place the pan or bowl over a pan of simmering water, and continue whisking until the custard is frothy and evenly coats the back of a spoon, 6–8 minutes. Do not let the upper container touch the hot water, or the zabaglione may curdle.

**3** Stir in the orange rind and serve the zabaglione immediately.

*LEFT: Tiramisù RIGHT: Zabaglione*

# CHOCOLATE RAVIOLI WITH WHITE CHOCOLATE FILLING

*Ravioli al Cioccolato*

his is a spectacular, sweet pasta, with cocoa powder added to the flour. The pasta packets contain a rich creamy filling.

### INGREDIENTS
*175g/6oz/1½ cups plain flour*
*pinch of salt*
*25g/1oz/¼ cup cocoa powder*
*30ml/2 tbsp icing sugar*
*2 large eggs*
*single cream and grated dark and white chocolate, to serve*

### FOR THE FILLING
*175g/6oz white chocolate*
*350g/12oz/3 cups cream cheese*
*1 egg, plus 1 beaten egg to seal*

### SERVES 4

---

### VARIATION
Use milk chocolate instead of white chocolate for the filling, and sprinkle the finished dish with grated milk chocolate.

---

1 Put the flour, salt, cocoa and icing sugar into a food processor, add the eggs, and process until the dough begins to come together. Tip out the dough and knead until smooth. Wrap and rest for 30 minutes.

2 To make the filling, break up the white chocolate into squares and melt it in a basin placed over a pan of barely simmering water. Cool slightly, then beat into the cream cheese with the egg. Spoon into a piping bag fitted with a plain nozzle.

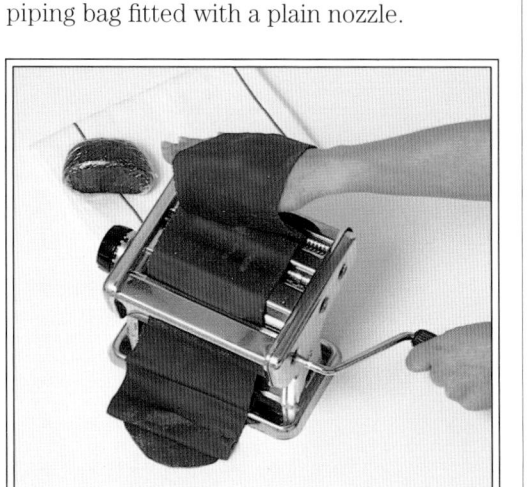

3 Cut the dough in half and wrap one portion in clear film. Roll out the pasta thinly to a rectangle on a lightly floured surface, or use a pasta machine. Cover with a clean, damp dish towel and repeat with the remaining pasta.

4 Pipe small mounds (about 5ml/1 tsp) of filling in even rows, spacing them at 4cm/1½in intervals, across one piece of the dough. Using a pastry brush, brush the spaces of dough between the mounds with beaten egg.

5 Using a rolling pin, lift the remaining sheet of pasta over the dough with the filling. Press down firmly between the pockets of filling, pushing out any trapped air. Cut into rounds with a serrated ravioli cutter or sharp knife. Transfer to a floured dish towel. Cover and rest for 1 hour.

6 Bring a large pan of water to the boil and add the ravioli a few at a time, stirring to prevent them sticking together. Simmer gently for 3–5 minutes, then remove with a slotted spoon. Serve with a generous splash of single cream and some grated chocolate.

# INDEX

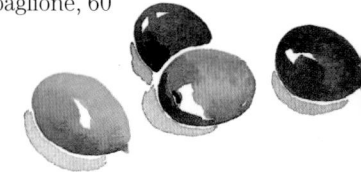